SPACE
SCIENCE FAIR
PROJECTS

JORDAN MCGILL

MEDIA ENHANCED BOOKS
AV2 BY WEIGL
ADDED VALUE · AUDIO VISUAL

www.av2books.com

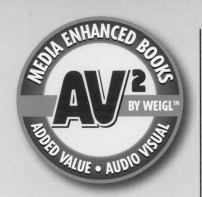

AV[2] provides enriched content that supplements and complements this book Weigl's AV[2] books strive to create inspired learning and engage young minds in a total learning experience.

Your AV[2] Media Enhanced books come alive with...

Audio
Listen to sections of the book read aloud.

Key Words
Study vocabulary, and complete a matching word activity.

Go to **www.av2books.com**, and enter this book's unique code.

Video
Watch informative video clips.

Quizzes
Test your knowledge.

BOOK CODE

X829455

Embedded Weblinks
Gain additional information for research.

Slide Show
View images and captions, and prepare a presentation.

AV[2] by Weigl brings you media enhanced books that support active learning.

Try This!
Complete activities and hands-on experiments.

... and much, much more!

Published by AV[2] by Weigl Publishers Inc.
350 5th Avenue, 59th Floor
New York, NY 10118
Website: www.av2books.com   www.weigl.com

Library of Congress Cataloging-in-Publication Data

McGill, Jordan.
 Space science fair projects / Jordan McGill.
    p. cm. -- (Science fair projects)
 Includes index.
 ISBN 978-1-61690-653-5 (hardcover : alk. paper) -- ISBN 978-1-61690-657-3 (softcover : alk. paper) -- ISBN 978-1-61690-331-2 (online)
 1. Astronomy--Experiments--Juvenile literature. 2. Science--Methodology--Juvenile literature. 3. Science projects--Juvenile literature. 4. Science fairs--Juvenile literature. I. Title.
 QB46.M15 2012
 520.78--dc22
                        2011014124

Printed in the United States of America in North Mankato, Minnesota
1 2 3 4 5 6 7 8 9 0 15 14 13 12 11

Project Coordinator Jordan McGill
Art Director Terry Paulhus

052011
WEP290411

Every reasonable effort has been made to trace ownership and to obtain permission to reprint copyright material. The publishers would be pleased to have any errors or omissions brought to their attention so that they may be corrected in subsequent printings.

Weigl acknowledges Getty Images as its primary image supplier for this title.

CONTENTS

Take Part in a Science Fair

WHAT IS A SCIENCE FAIR?

A science fair is an event where students use the **scientific method** to create projects. These projects are then presented to spectators. Judges examine each project and award prizes for following the scientific method and preparing detailed displays. Some science fair winners move on to compete at larger fairs.

WHY SHOULD YOU TAKE PART IN A SCIENCE FAIR?

Science fairs are an excellent way to learn about topics that interest you. Winning is not the only reason to compete at a science fair. Science fairs are an opportunity for you to work hard on a project and show it off. You will also get to see the projects other students are presenting and learn from them as well.

ANYTHING ELSE I SHOULD KNOW?

Before you start, you should begin a logbook. A logbook is a handwritten diary of the tasks you performed to complete your science fair project. Include any problems or interesting events that occur.

WHERE DO I FIND A SCIENCE FAIR?

There are many fairs around the country and worldwide. Ask your teacher if he or she knows if any science fairs are held in your city. Once you find a fair to compete in, you can start preparing your project.

Eight Steps to a Great Science Fair Project

STEP 1
Select a topic

To begin, you must select a topic. Choose a topic that you would like to learn about. That way, working on the project will be exciting.

STEP 2
Form a question about your topic

Think of a question you have about your topic. You can ask, "Why do stars **twinkle**?", or, "Can the Sun be used to tell time?"

STEP 3
Research your question

Visit a library, and go online to research your topic. Keep track of where you found your **sources** and who wrote them. Most of your time should be spent learning about your topic.

STEP 4
Think about the answer to your question

Form a **hypothesis** that may answer your question. The sentence, "Stars twinkle because their light is **refracted** by Earth's atmosphere" is a hypothesis.

STEP 5
Plan an experiment to test your hypothesis

Design an **experiment** that you can repeat and that has observable **reactions**. Make a detailed plan of what you will do in your experiment and what materials you will need. Also include what you will be looking for when you do your experiment.

STEP 6
Conduct your experiment and record data

Carry out your experiment, and carefully observe what happens. Take notes. Record **data** if you need to. If you have nothing to note or record, reconsider whether your experiment has observable reactions.

STEP 7
Draw conclusions from your data

Were your predictions right? Sometimes, your hypothesis will be proven wrong. That is fine. The goal is to find the truth, not to be correct. When wrong, scientists think of a new hypothesis and try again.

STEP 8
Prepare a report and display

Write a report that explains your project. Include the topic, question, materials, plan, predictions, data, and **conclusion** in your report. Create a display that you can show at the science fair.

Picking a Space Science Topic

Space science is the study of space and the objects in it. There are many types of scientists who study space, including **astronomers** and **physicists**. They look at planets in distant **galaxies**, develop **theories** on how the **universe** began, and design technology that can take people beyond Earth's limits.

This book offers sample experiments for each of the six earth science topics listed below. These experiments can be used to develop a science fair project. Select a topic that interests you. Then, use the sample experiment in this book for your project. You can also think of your own experiment that fits the topic.

TOPIC 1 THE MOON

The Moon is an object that orbits Earth. It is the only place in space, other than Earth, that humans have been. The Moon is studied to learn how it came to be and to see if humans could adapt to one day live there.

TOPIC 2 PLANETS

Earth is one of many trillion **planets**. There are seven other planets in our **solar system**. Scientists study these planets and search for planets in other space systems as well. They hope to find planets that can support life.

TOPIC 3 ROCKETS

Rockets are used to launch objects from Earth into space. Scientists develop new designs for rockets. They try to build rockets that can carry objects into deep space.

TOPIC 4 STARS

Stars are massive balls of fiery gas that burn for billions of years. Many are larger than the Sun in our solar system. Scientists study stars to learn more about the universe and the role that stars play in it.

TOPIC 5 THE SUN

The Sun supports life on Earth by providing light, heat, and energy. It is much like other stars, except that it is the closest one to Earth. By examining the Sun, people can learn more about life on Earth.

TOPIC 6 TELESCOPES

Without telescopes, many distant planets and stars would be almost impossible to see. Telescopes are an essential tool for anyone interested in space. From backyard astronomers to scientists working in billion-dollar facilities, telescopes allow those looking to the sky to see much more.

How Powerful are Asteroids?

Background Information

Many planets have moons. In fact, most planets have more than one moon. Jupiter has 63 moons. Earth, however, has only one moon.

The Moon is actually made of rocks. These rocks are much like the rocks on Earth. One theory of the Moon's origin says that an **asteroid** struck Earth billions of years ago. The asteroid chipped a large chunk off Earth. This piece of rock began to **orbit** around Earth. It became the Moon that humans see glowing in the sky.

EXPERIMENT

A steroids range from the size of a boulder to more than 100 miles (200 kilometers) across. Some of these larger chunks have collided with the Moon's surface. Their impact has created craters in the Moon's surface. Many of these craters stretch for miles (km). One of the Moon's largest craters is more than 25 miles (40 km) across.

The Moon's distinct cratered landscape has been shaped by millions of years of collisions. In this experiment, you will learn how asteroid size affects the diameter and shape of a crater.

TIP #1
You could drop a pebble from different heights to model how speed affects the size of crater created.

TIP #2
What happens if you lightly lob the pebble sideways, instead of dropping it straight down? Think about how asteroids striking the Moon from an angle would affect the landscape.

Make Craters in 6 steps

CAUTION

Messy

DIFFICULTY

EASY   MEDIUM   HARD

TIME 30 minutes

MATERIALS

- Large tray or box that is at least 1 square foot (.09 square meters)
- Bag of flour
- Cocoa powder
- Ruler
- 5 small pebbles of different sizes

INSTRUCTIONS

STEP 1 Fill the tray or box with flour so that it is 1 to 2 inches (2.5 centimeters) deep.

STEP 2 Sprinkle a thin layer of cocoa powder on top of the flour.

STEP 3 Measure the diameter of each pebble. Record this information for later.

STEP 4 Drop the smallest pebble into the flour from a height of about 3 feet (.91 meters) above the tray.

STEP 5 Measure the diameter of the **crater** the pebble makes in the flour. Also, note how deep it is.

STEP 6 Aim for a different area of the tray, and drop the next largest pebble. Repeat steps 5 and 6 for all of the pebbles. How does the size of the pebble affect the diameter and depth of the crater?

Which Planets Can Best Support Life?

Background Information

Earth is one of eight planets in our solar system. The eight planets in order from the Sun are Mercury, Venus, Earth, Mars, Jupiter, Saturn, Uranus, and Neptune. All of these planets, including Earth, orbit the Sun.

Earth, Mars, Mercury, and Venus are called terrestrial planets. They are made mainly of rock. Jupiter, Neptune, Saturn, and Uranus are made up mostly of gas. They are called gas giants.

EXPERIMENT

Earth has all the necessary requirements to support life. It is the perfect distance from the Sun. It is not too hot and not too cold. Its atmosphere supports **organisms** that produce oxygen.

Other than Earth though, which planet has the safest environment for human life? In this experiment, you will study the other planets of the solar system and decide what the next safest planet is. Important factors to consider are day and night cycles, climate, and atmosphere.

TIP #1
No planet in our solar system other than Earth will meet all the requirements for human life. Find the best alternative.

TIP #2
In the "Other" column, record information that does not fit under the other headings.

Find Habitable Planets in 4 steps

DIFFICULTY

TIME 2 HOURS

MATERIALS
- Pencil
- Paper
- Access to research tools

INSTRUCTIONS

STEP 1 Prepare a table. The table will have seven columns and eight rows. In the first column, record each planet in the solar system other than Earth. Along the top row, write Planets, Average Day Temperature, Average Night Temperature, Atmosphere, Average Wind Speed, Water Availability, and Other.

STEP 2 Using a library and the Internet, do a quick search on what makes Earth able to support life. Use the categories on your chart as guidelines. Take notes on your findings, and save them for later.

STEP 3 Do the same research for each of the other planets. Organize your research by placing your findings in the table.

STEP 4 Using your notes from steps 2 and 3, compare Earth to the other planets. Decide which planet shares the most features with Earth. Could humans live on this planet? Why or why not?

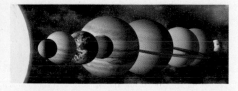

How Do Rockets Lift Off From Earth?

Background Information

A rocket is a powerful way to launch things over great distances. There are many types of rockets. Most rockets are tube-shaped devices that carry a special type of **fuel**, as well as oxygen to burn the fuel. Together, fuel and oxygen are called the **propellants**. They create the **thrust** to move the rocket. When the fuel is ignited, gases are released. The force of these gases pushing in one direction causes the tube to move through the air in the opposite direction. On Earth, there is oxygen all around us, but there is almost no oxygen in space. Rockets are able to work in space because they carry their own oxygen with them.

EXPERIMENT

Sir Isaac Newton discovered, "For every action there is an equal and opposite reaction." In a rocket, that means, when the hot gases rush out of the opening at the bottom, an equal force pushes the rocket in the opposite direction.

Create an experiment that demonstrates Newton's law without using dangerous fuels. Instead of rocket propellant, this experiment uses a baking soda and vinegar reaction to launch the rocket high in the air.

TIP #1
Decorate your rocket with markers or crayons to make it look accurate.

TIP #2
It is best to perform this experiment outside. You want to avoid breaking objects in your house.

Make a Rocket in **7** Steps

CAUTION

Messy   Watch Out   Sharp

DIFFICULTY

EASY   MEDIUM   HARD

TIME 30 minutes

MATERIALS
- Two pieces of white paper
- Tape
- Small plastic film canister
- Scissors
- Baking soda
- 2 tablespoons of vinegar

INSTRUCTIONS

STEP 1 Roll a piece of paper around the film canister so that the bottom edge is flush with the edge of the canister. Be sure to leave the side with the lid on the bottom.

STEP 2 Tape the paper tightly so that it stays on the canister. You should be able to place the lid back on the canister.

STEP 3 Form a cone for the rocket. To do so, cut a circle from the other piece of paper. Then, cut a pizza-shaped slice out of the circle. Roll the slice to make the cone. Attach it to the top of the rocket with tape.

STEP 4 Cut out two triangles from the leftover paper. These will be your rocket's fins. Attach them to the sides of the canister with tape.

STEP 5 Stuff the film canister with baking soda. Be sure to pack it tightly.

STEP 6 Add two tablespoons of vinegar to the film canister. Seal the lid quickly and tightly.

STEP 7 Place the rocket on the floor with the canister lid facing down. Step back, and watch out. The vinegar reacts with the baking soda and causes the rocket to blast off.

Why Do Stars Twinkle?

Background Information

The night sky is dotted with tiny, twinkling stars. All stars appear small from Earth because they are so far away. In fact, stars are very large. Many stars are larger than the Sun.

Stars are huge, glowing balls of swirling gases. These gases interact to produce energy. Some of this energy is released in the form of heat, and some is released in the form of light. Stars use up all of their gases over time. They grow dimmer and cooler as a result. After billions of years, they stop glowing, fade out, and die.

EXPERIMENT

When you look into the sky and see something bright, you can tell if you are looking at star. Only stars twinkle. This twinkling occurs because a star's light is bent in many different directions by Earth's atmosphere. This causes the star's brightness and size to look like it is changing rapidly.

In this experiment, you will learn about stars twinkling. You will also examine how light affects star watching.

TIP #1
In your report, be sure to include reasons for your findings. Like all science fair projects, research is important.

TIP #2
Astronomers use the term "seeing" to describe how well they can examine something in the sky.

Find Stars in 5 Steps

CAUTION

Adult's Help

DIFFICULTY

EASY   MEDIUM   HARD

TIME 30 minutes

MATERIALS
- Stopwatch
- Notepad
- Paper

INSTRUCTIONS

STEP 1 On a night when stars are visible, go outside with an adult, and take a look at the night sky. Find a star to focus on. Remember that only stars twinkle.

STEP 2 Set your stopwatch for 10 seconds, and count how many times the star blinks in that time.

STEP 3 Now, find two more stars. One should be high in the sky, and the other should be lower. Which twinkles more? To find out, perform a 10-second blink count on each. Do a few tests to make sure your **observations** are accurate. Record your results.

STEP 4 Look at another star. Does it change color as it twinkles? Do some stars change color more? Are the stars that change color the most high up or low? Record your answer.

STEP 5 Which stars twinkled the most? Try to find out what factors make stars twinkle more or less. You may notice other factors that affect how much stars twinkle. Use your notes to figure out the best conditions for seeing stars. The less twinkling, the better a star can be observed. Your work can help other star watchers.

How Can We Tell Time by the Sun?

Background Information

The Sun is a star. It looks different from the other stars in the sky because it is so much closer to Earth than any other star. The Sun is the brightest object visible from Earth. It provides Earth with light and heat. There would be no life on Earth without the Sun's energy.

The Sun's heat has to travel a great distance to warm Earth. To provide Earth with its heat, the Sun itself must be even hotter. The temperature of the Sun's surface is about 10,000° Fahrenheit (5,538° Celsius). It is even hotter above and below the surface of the Sun. The Sun's core is about 27 million° Fahrenheit (15 million° C).

EXPERIMENT

All planets orbit counterclockwise around the Sun. The time that it takes a planet to complete a full orbit is the length of its year. Mercury takes only 88 Earth days to travel around the Sun. One year on Mars is almost as long as two Earth years.

As planets move around the Sun, they spin. This causes day and night cycles. In this way, the Sun helps people determine what time of day it is. This experiment shows how the Sun can be used to tell time.

TIP #1

In ancient times, people did not have access to watches. They created **sundials** to tell time.

TIP #2

Be careful not to move the cup once you set it up. Draw a circle around the cup, and put a point facing north. If the cup is moved, you can put it back.

Tell Time in 7 Steps

DIFFICULTY

EASY   MEDIUM   HARD

TIME 30 minutes + 7 hours of observation

MATERIALS
- A compass
- A fast food drinking cup with a lid
- A straw
- Tape
- A permanent marker
- Watch

INSTRUCTIONS

STEP 1 Punch a hole in the side of the cup about 2 inches (5 centimeters) from the top. Then, place something in the cup to weigh it down. Fasten the lid to the top.

STEP 2 Push the straw through the hole in the lid and out the hole in the side of the cup.

STEP 3 Tape the straw to the side of the cup. You have now made a sundial.

STEP 4 On a sunny day, find a spot that does not have any buildings or trees blocking the Sun. Put the sundial on a flat surface.

STEP 5 Use the compass to find out which direction is north. Point the straw in that direction.

STEP 6 At 10:00 a.m., draw a mark on the lid of the cup to show where the straw's shadow falls. At 11:00 a.m., draw another mark on the lid. Do so every hour until 5:00 p.m.

STEP 7 You can now use your sundial to tell time. Be aware, however, that your sundial has to be rotated with the seasons to compensate for the Sun's changing arc across the sky. At noon, the Sun should be almost straight overhead of the sundial. If it is not, you will have to make the necessary adjustments.

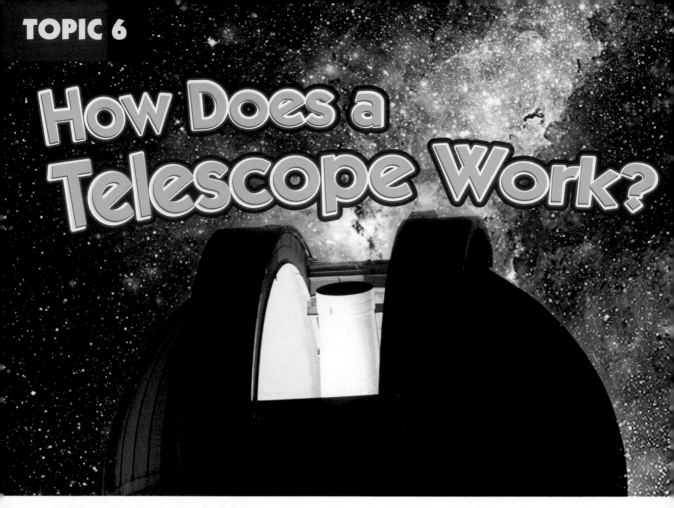

How Does a Telescope Work?

Background Information

Astronomers use telescopes to help them see stars and other space objects. Telescopes magnify distant objects. They allow the human eye to see farther than it can on its own. Telescopes can do so because they collect more light than the human eye.

Details of the Moon's surface are difficult to see. A telescope can show much more of the Moon's surface, including the details of its mountains, valleys, and craters. Larger and more powerful telescopes have been developed over time. Planets, stars, and entire galaxies can now be observed through telescopes.

There are two main types of telescopes. A refracting telescope has two lenses. One lens collects the light of an object. The other lens magnifies the image so that it is clear. A reflecting telescope, on the other hand, uses a mirror to collect the light of an object in the sky. The light then bounces off the mirror and onto a lens.

EXPERIMENT

n this experiment, you will construct a refracting telescope. Although your telescope will be less powerful than the large ones astronomers use, you may be able to help make important discoveries. Amateur space watchers have found small asteroids between Mars and Jupiter. They have also discovered **comets**.

Craft a Telescope in **4** Steps

TIP #1

You could make a telescope with a focus using two tubes. Place one lens on the bottom of one of the tubes and the other lens on the top of the other tube. Insert the bottom tube into the top tube. You can slide the two tubes together and apart to focus.

TIP #2

When you glue the lenses into the cardboard tube, be sure that the lenses are straight. If they are angled, the telescope will not work properly.

CAUTION

Cost   Sharp

DIFFICULTY

EASY   MEDIUM   HARD

TIME 30 minutes

MATERIALS
- Cardboard paper tube
- Glue
- Cardboard
- Large convex lens
- Small concave lens
- Scissors
- Ruler

INSTRUCTIONS

STEP 1 Hold the larger lens in front of the smaller one. Put both of them in front of you, and look through them. Experiment with the distance between the lenses. When the objects in front of you come into focus, record the distance between the lenses.

STEP 2 Cut the paper towel tube so that it is slightly longer than the distance you discovered in Step 1. It is best to have one extra inch (2.5 cm) of tube.

STEP 3 Glue the convex lens inside the tube near the bottom. Leave half an inch (1.3 cm) of room so that you can comfortably look through it.

STEP 4 Glue the concave lens inside the tube near the top. Leave half an inch of room on this end as well to protect the lens. Look through your telescope at the night sky. Can you see farther into the sky? How much more can you see using the telescope?

Preparing Your Report

Once your experiment is completed, write a report. The purpose of the report is to summarize your work. You want others to understand the question, the research, and the experiment. The report also explains your results and ties everything together in a conclusion.

1 ### Title
The title of your report should be the question you are trying to answer.

2 ### Purpose
This section of the report should include a few sentences explaining why you chose this project.

3 ### Hypothesis
The hypothesis is made up of one sentence that explains the answer your experiment was meant to prove.

4 ### Background
Write a summary of the information you found during your research. You most likely will not need to use all of your research.

5 ### Materials
Write a list of the materials you used during your experiment. This is the same as the list of materials included with each sample experiment in this book.

6 ### Plan
Write out the steps needed to carry out your experiment.

7 ### Results
Write all observations and relevant data you recorded during your experiment here. Include any tables or graphs you made.

8 ### Conclusion
In this part of the report, state what you learned. Be sure to writ how you think your results prove or disprove your hypothesis. You should also write your hypothes again somewhere in this section It is acceptable if your hypothes was false. What is important is that you were creative and followed the scientific method

9 ### Bibliography
Include an alphabetical list by the author's last name of all sources you used.

Making Your Display

Most science fairs encourage the use of a backboard to display your project. Most displays use a three-panel backboard. It stands up on its own and is easy to view.

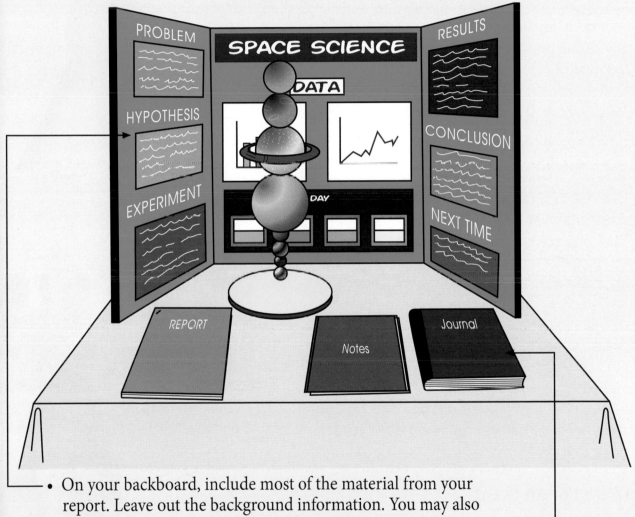

- On your backboard, include most of the material from your report. Leave out the background information. You may also include photos or drawings to help explain your project.

- Most often, your backboard will be placed on a table. On the table, you can include any models you created or samples you collected. Also include the logbook and a copy of your report.

- If possible, you may also perform your experiment at the fair.

Impressing the Judges

Know the Rules

Judges expect that you know the rules. Breaking rules can lead to lost points and even **disqualification**. Rules will change depending on who is organizing the science fair. Before you begin your project, talk to the organizers of the fair you plan to compete in. Ask them for a list of rules.

* Most fairs do not allow any dangerous materials, such as flames and organisms that could make someone sick.

Practice Presenting

To stand out at the science fair, you have to give a strong presentation to the judges. Write a short speech that covers what you want to say. Your speech should summarize why you chose the project. It should also explain the experiment and your conclusions. Practice this speech until you are comfortable. Speak confidently and clearly.

* Many judges will ask questions. Present your project to friends and family. Then, have them ask questions as if they were judges.

Dress For an Event

A science fair is a special event. It is different from an ordinary day. When you go somewhere special, do your parents have you dress up? Judges look at every part of your presentation, including you. Wear something special. Comb your hair. Tuck in your shirt. Tie your shoes. You are presenting yourself as much as your project.

Glossary

asteroid: small, usually irregularly shaped body orbiting the Sun

astronomers: researchers who study space

comets: frozen, pieces of dust and gas that revolve around the Sun

conclusion: the results or outcomes of an act or process

crater: a bowl-shaped pit in a surface made by the impact of a body, such as an asteroid

data: items of information

disqualification: to be eliminated from a competition

experiment: a test, trial, or procedure

fuel: a material that produces heat or power

galaxies: a system of millions or billions of stars

hypothesis: a possible explanation for a scientific question

observations: information noted while carefully watching something

orbit: the curved path of a planet around a space body, such as the Sun

organisms: any living things

physicists: experts in physics

planets: large objects in space that orbit a star

propellants: materials, such as explosive charges or rocket fuel, that move an object

reactions: when two or more substances combine to make a new chemical substance

refracted: deflected light from a straight path

scientific method: a system of observation

solar system: the Sun together with the eight planets and all other bodies that orbit it

sources: the books or websites from which research was obtained

sundial: a tool that shows the time using the Sun

theories: systems of ideas that explain how something works

thrust: the forward-directed force developed in a jet or rocket engine

twinkle: a light that switches from bright to faint repeatedly

universe: the space that contains all matter and energy in existence

Index

Log on to www.av2books.com

AV[2] by Weigl brings you media enhanced books that support active learning. Go to www.av2books.com, and enter the special code found on page 2 of this book. You will gain access to enriched and enhanced content that supplements and complements this book. Content includes video, audio, web links, quizzes, a slide show, and activities.

Audio
Listen to sections of the book read aloud.

Video
Watch informative video clips.

Embedded Weblinks
Gain additional information for research.

Try This!
Complete activities and hands-on experiments.

WHAT'S ONLINE?

Try This!	Embedded Weblinks	Video	EXTRA FEATURES
Create useful observation sheets.	Check out more information about space science topics.	Watch a video about space science.	**Audio** Listen to sections of the book read aloud.
Make a judging sheet.	Learn how to coordinate a science fair.	Check out another video about space science.	**Key Words** Study vocabulary, and complete a matching word activity.
Make a timeline to make sure projects are finished on time.	Learn more about creating an effective display.		**Slide Show** View images and caption and prepare a presentatic
Complete fun interactive space science activities.			**Quizzes** Test your knowledge.

AV[2] was built to bridge the gap between print and digital. We encourage you to tell us what you like and what you want to see in the future.
Sign up to be an AV[2] Ambassador at www.av2books.com/ambassador.